50 Decadent Chocolate Desserts

By: Kelly Johnson

Table of Contents

- Chocolate Lava Cake
- Chocolate Mousse
- Chocolate Truffles
- Flourless Chocolate Cake
- Chocolate Fondue
- Chocolate Soufflé
- Chocolate Brownies
- Chocolate Cheesecake
- Chocolate Tarts
- Chocolate Panna Cotta
- Chocolate Cupcakes
- Chocolate Fudge
- Chocolate Ice Cream
- Chocolate-Dipped Strawberries
- Chocolate Chip Cookies
- Chocolate Eclairs
- Chocolate Ganache Tart
- Chocolate Caramel Tart
- Chocolate Cream Pie
- Chocolate Clafoutis
- Chocolate Swirl Cheesecake
- Chocolate Pudding
- Chocolate-Dipped Pretzels
- Chocolate-Peanut Butter Cups
- Chocolate-Pecan Pie
- Chocolate-Coconut Bars
- Chocolate-Dipped Marshmallows
- Chocolate Meringue Pie
- Chocolate Pots de Crème
- Triple Chocolate Cake
- Chocolate Croissants
- Chocolate Almond Biscotti
- Chocolate Babka
- Chocolate Chip Scones
- Chocolate Peanut Butter Pie

- Chocolate Hazelnut Mousse
- Chocolate Caramel Brownies
- Chocolate and Raspberry Tart
- Chocolate-Pistachio Tart
- Chocolate Lava Cookies
- Chocolate Ricotta Cake
- Chocolate Churros
- Chocolate Banana Bread
- Chocolate Tiramisu
- Chocolate-Coffee Cake
- Chocolate and Mint Cupcakes
- Chocolate Coconut Macaroons
- Chocolate Layer Cake
- Chocolate Fudge Brownies with Walnuts
- Chocolate Soufflé Cake

Chocolate Lava Cake

Ingredients:

- 200g dark chocolate (70% cocoa)
- 100g butter
- 3 large eggs
- 3 large egg yolks
- 75g sugar
- 1 tsp vanilla extract
- 50g all-purpose flour
- Pinch of salt
- Butter (for greasing)
- Cocoa powder (for dusting)

Instructions:

1. Preheat the oven to 200°C (400°F). Grease four ramekins and dust with cocoa powder.
2. Melt the chocolate and butter in a heatproof bowl over simmering water.
3. Whisk eggs, egg yolks, sugar, and vanilla in a separate bowl until thick.
4. Gently fold in the melted chocolate and sifted flour.
5. Pour batter into ramekins and bake for 12–14 minutes. The edges should be set, but the center should be soft.
6. Let it cool for 1 minute, then invert onto plates. Serve with vanilla ice cream or fresh berries.

Chocolate Mousse

Ingredients:

- 200g dark chocolate
- 300ml heavy cream
- 2 tbsp sugar
- 1 tsp vanilla extract
- 2 large egg whites

Instructions:

1. Melt chocolate in a heatproof bowl over simmering water.
2. Whisk the cream with sugar and vanilla until soft peaks form.
3. In another bowl, beat egg whites until stiff peaks form.
4. Gently fold the melted chocolate into the whipped cream, then fold in the egg whites.
5. Spoon mousse into serving glasses and refrigerate for 2 hours before serving.

Chocolate Truffles

Ingredients:

- 200g dark chocolate (70% cocoa)
- 100ml heavy cream
- 1 tsp vanilla extract
- Cocoa powder, chopped nuts, or melted chocolate (for coating)

Instructions:

1. Heat cream in a saucepan until it just starts to simmer. Pour over chopped chocolate and let it sit for 1 minute.
2. Stir gently until smooth, then add vanilla extract.
3. Refrigerate the mixture for 2–3 hours until firm enough to roll into balls.
4. Roll truffles in cocoa powder, nuts, or melted chocolate. Refrigerate until set.

Flourless Chocolate Cake

Ingredients:

- 200g dark chocolate (70% cocoa)
- 200g butter
- 200g sugar
- 5 large eggs
- 1 tsp vanilla extract
- 1 pinch of salt

Instructions:

1. Preheat the oven to 180°C (350°F). Grease and line a 9-inch round cake pan.
2. Melt the chocolate and butter together in a heatproof bowl over simmering water.
3. Whisk sugar, eggs, vanilla, and salt until smooth.
4. Stir in the melted chocolate mixture and pour into the prepared pan.
5. Bake for 25-30 minutes. The cake should be firm on top but soft in the center.
6. Let it cool completely before serving with whipped cream or berries.

Chocolate Fondue

Ingredients:

- 200g dark chocolate
- 100ml heavy cream
- 1 tbsp sugar (optional)
- 1 tsp vanilla extract
- Fresh fruit, marshmallows, or cubed cake for dipping

Instructions:

1. Melt the chocolate and cream in a fondue pot or a heatproof bowl over simmering water.
2. Stir in sugar and vanilla extract.
3. Serve immediately with dippable items like strawberries, marshmallows, or cubed cake.

Chocolate Soufflé

Ingredients:

- 100g dark chocolate
- 50g butter
- 3 large eggs, separated
- 50g sugar
- 1 tsp vanilla extract
- Pinch of salt

Instructions:

1. Preheat the oven to 180°C (350°F). Butter and sugar ramekins.
2. Melt chocolate and butter together in a heatproof bowl over simmering water.
3. Whisk egg yolks with half of the sugar and vanilla until pale.
4. In a separate bowl, beat egg whites with the remaining sugar and salt until stiff peaks form.
5. Fold the melted chocolate mixture into the egg yolk mixture, then gently fold in the egg whites.
6. Spoon the mixture into ramekins and bake for 12–15 minutes until puffed and set. Serve immediately.

Chocolate Brownies

Ingredients:

- 200g dark chocolate (70% cocoa)
- 150g butter
- 200g sugar
- 3 large eggs
- 1 tsp vanilla extract
- 100g flour
- 1/2 tsp salt

Instructions:

1. Preheat the oven to 180°C (350°F). Grease and line a 9-inch square baking pan.
2. Melt chocolate and butter together in a heatproof bowl over simmering water.
3. Whisk sugar, eggs, and vanilla in a separate bowl until combined.
4. Stir in the melted chocolate mixture and flour, then pour into the prepared pan.
5. Bake for 20–25 minutes until a toothpick inserted comes out with a few moist crumbs.
6. Let it cool before cutting into squares.

Chocolate Cheesecake

Ingredients:

For the crust:

- 200g digestive biscuits, crushed
- 100g melted butter
- 2 tbsp sugar

For the filling:

- 500g cream cheese, softened
- 200g dark chocolate, melted
- 200g sugar
- 3 large eggs
- 1 tsp vanilla extract

Instructions:

1. Preheat the oven to 180°C (350°F). Mix crushed biscuits, butter, and sugar, then press into the base of a springform pan.
2. Beat cream cheese with sugar until smooth. Stir in melted chocolate, eggs, and vanilla.
3. Pour the filling over the crust and bake for 45–50 minutes until set.
4. Let it cool completely before refrigerating for at least 4 hours. Serve with whipped cream or chocolate ganache.

Chocolate Tarts

Ingredients:

For the crust:

- 200g digestive biscuits or graham crackers, crushed
- 100g melted butter
- 2 tbsp sugar

For the filling:

- 200g dark chocolate (70% cocoa)
- 200ml heavy cream
- 2 tbsp sugar
- 1 tsp vanilla extract

Instructions:

1. Preheat the oven to 180°C (350°F). Combine crushed biscuits, melted butter, and sugar. Press the mixture into tart pans.
2. Bake the crust for 8-10 minutes, then let it cool.
3. For the filling, heat cream and sugar in a pan until it starts to simmer. Pour over chopped chocolate and let it sit for 1-2 minutes, then stir until smooth.
4. Pour the chocolate mixture into the cooled tart crusts. Refrigerate for at least 2 hours before serving.

Chocolate Panna Cotta

Ingredients:

- 200g dark chocolate
- 500ml heavy cream
- 50g sugar
- 2 tsp vanilla extract
- 2 tsp gelatin powder
- 2 tbsp water

Instructions:

1. In a small bowl, dissolve gelatin in water and let it sit for 5 minutes.
2. Heat cream and sugar in a saucepan until warm. Stir in chopped chocolate and vanilla until smooth.
3. Add the dissolved gelatin to the mixture and stir until fully combined.
4. Pour into serving glasses and refrigerate for 4 hours or overnight. Serve with berries or whipped cream.

Chocolate Cupcakes

Ingredients:

- 200g all-purpose flour
- 100g cocoa powder
- 1 tsp baking powder
- 1 tsp baking soda
- 200g sugar
- 2 eggs
- 240ml milk
- 120ml vegetable oil
- 1 tsp vanilla extract
- 240ml boiling water
- A pinch of salt

For the frosting:

- 200g dark chocolate
- 200g butter
- 2 tbsp heavy cream
- 100g powdered sugar

Instructions:

1. Preheat the oven to 180°C (350°F) and line a cupcake tin with paper liners.
2. Mix flour, cocoa powder, baking powder, baking soda, sugar, and salt in a bowl.
3. Add eggs, milk, oil, and vanilla, then beat until smooth.
4. Gradually add boiling water to the batter until combined.
5. Pour batter into cupcake liners and bake for 18–20 minutes.
6. For the frosting, melt chocolate and butter together, then whisk in heavy cream and powdered sugar.
7. Once the cupcakes cool, frost with the chocolate icing and enjoy!

Chocolate Fudge

Ingredients:

- 400g dark chocolate (70% cocoa)
- 1 can (400g) sweetened condensed milk
- 50g butter
- 1 tsp vanilla extract

Instructions:

1. Line a square baking pan with parchment paper.
2. In a saucepan, melt the chocolate, sweetened condensed milk, and butter over low heat, stirring frequently.
3. Stir in the vanilla extract.
4. Pour the mixture into the prepared pan and spread it out evenly.
5. Refrigerate for 2-3 hours or until set, then cut into squares.

Chocolate Ice Cream

Ingredients:

- 200g dark chocolate
- 500ml heavy cream
- 200ml whole milk
- 100g sugar
- 4 large egg yolks
- 1 tsp vanilla extract

Instructions:

1. In a heatproof bowl, melt the chocolate over simmering water.
2. In a saucepan, heat milk and cream until it begins to simmer.
3. Whisk egg yolks and sugar together in a separate bowl. Gradually pour the hot cream mixture into the egg yolks, whisking constantly.
4. Return the mixture to the saucepan and cook on low heat until it thickens. Stir in melted chocolate and vanilla.
5. Chill the mixture for 4 hours, then churn it in an ice cream maker according to the manufacturer's instructions. Freeze until firm.

Chocolate-Dipped Strawberries

Ingredients:

- 200g dark chocolate
- 12-15 fresh strawberries

Instructions:

1. Melt the chocolate in a heatproof bowl over simmering water.
2. Dip each strawberry into the melted chocolate, coating about two-thirds of the berry.
3. Place dipped strawberries on parchment paper and refrigerate for 30 minutes to set.
4. Serve immediately or store in the fridge.

Chocolate Chip Cookies

Ingredients:

- 200g all-purpose flour
- 100g brown sugar
- 100g white sugar
- 1 tsp baking soda
- ½ tsp salt
- 120g butter, softened
- 2 large eggs
- 1 tsp vanilla extract
- 200g chocolate chips

Instructions:

1. Preheat the oven to 180°C (350°F). Line baking sheets with parchment paper.
2. Cream together butter, brown sugar, and white sugar.
3. Beat in eggs and vanilla.
4. In another bowl, mix flour, baking soda, and salt. Gradually add to the butter mixture.
5. Stir in chocolate chips.
6. Drop spoonfuls of dough onto the baking sheet and bake for 8-10 minutes.

Chocolate Eclairs

Ingredients:

For the choux pastry:

- 100g butter
- 250ml water
- 150g all-purpose flour
- 4 large eggs
- 1 pinch of salt

For the filling:

- 300ml heavy cream
- 2 tbsp powdered sugar
- 1 tsp vanilla extract

For the glaze:

- 100g dark chocolate
- 2 tbsp butter

Instructions:

1. Preheat the oven to 200°C (400°F).
2. In a saucepan, melt butter in water and bring to a boil. Stir in flour and cook until the dough forms.
3. Remove from heat and beat in eggs one at a time.
4. Pipe the dough into long eclair shapes on a baking sheet and bake for 20-25 minutes.
5. Whisk cream, powdered sugar, and vanilla until soft peaks form. Fill eclairs with the whipped cream.
6. Melt chocolate and butter, then dip eclairs in the chocolate glaze. Let them set before serving.

Chocolate Ganache Tart

Ingredients:

For the crust:

- 200g digestive biscuits or graham crackers, crushed
- 100g melted butter

For the ganache filling:

- 300g dark chocolate (70% cocoa)
- 300ml heavy cream
- 2 tbsp sugar

Instructions:

1. Preheat the oven to 180°C (350°F). Press crushed biscuits mixed with melted butter into a tart pan. Bake for 10 minutes, then cool.
2. For the ganache, heat cream and sugar until it just begins to simmer. Pour over chopped chocolate and stir until smooth.
3. Pour the ganache into the cooled crust and refrigerate for at least 2 hours to set.
4. Serve chilled, garnished with berries or whipped cream.

Chocolate Caramel Tart

Ingredients:

For the crust:

- 200g digestive biscuits or graham crackers, crushed
- 100g melted butter

For the caramel filling:

- 200g brown sugar
- 100g butter
- 200ml heavy cream
- 1 tsp vanilla extract
- Pinch of salt

For the chocolate ganache:

- 200g dark chocolate (70% cocoa)
- 200ml heavy cream

Instructions:

1. Preheat the oven to 180°C (350°F). Press crushed biscuits mixed with melted butter into a tart pan. Bake for 10 minutes, then cool.
2. For the caramel filling, melt sugar and butter in a saucepan over medium heat. Once melted, add cream and vanilla, and simmer for 5 minutes. Stir in salt and pour over the cooled crust.
3. For the ganache, heat cream until it just starts to simmer, then pour over chopped chocolate. Stir until smooth and pour over the caramel layer.
4. Refrigerate for at least 2 hours before serving.

Chocolate Cream Pie

Ingredients:

For the crust:

- 200g graham cracker crumbs
- 100g melted butter
- 2 tbsp sugar

For the filling:

- 200g dark chocolate
- 500ml whole milk
- 4 large egg yolks
- 100g sugar
- 2 tbsp cornstarch
- 2 tbsp butter
- 1 tsp vanilla extract

For the topping:

- 250ml heavy cream
- 2 tbsp powdered sugar

Instructions:

1. Preheat the oven to 180°C (350°F). Combine graham cracker crumbs, melted butter, and sugar, then press into a pie dish. Bake for 10 minutes, then cool.
2. For the filling, melt chocolate in a saucepan. In another bowl, whisk milk, egg yolks, sugar, and cornstarch. Slowly add this mixture to the melted chocolate and cook on medium heat until thickened. Remove from heat, stir in butter and vanilla.
3. Pour the filling into the cooled crust and refrigerate for 4 hours.
4. Whip the heavy cream with powdered sugar and top the pie.

Chocolate Clafoutis

Ingredients:

- 200g dark chocolate (70% cocoa)
- 4 large eggs
- 100g sugar
- 250ml whole milk
- 50g all-purpose flour
- 1 tsp vanilla extract
- Pinch of salt

Instructions:

1. Preheat the oven to 180°C (350°F). Grease a baking dish.
2. Melt the chocolate in a heatproof bowl over simmering water.
3. In a separate bowl, whisk eggs, sugar, milk, flour, vanilla, and salt until smooth.
4. Pour the batter into the baking dish, then spoon melted chocolate in small dollops.
5. Bake for 25-30 minutes, until puffed and set. Serve warm.

Chocolate Swirl Cheesecake

Ingredients:

For the crust:

- 200g graham cracker crumbs
- 100g melted butter
- 2 tbsp sugar

For the filling:

- 500g cream cheese, softened
- 200g dark chocolate
- 200g sugar
- 4 large eggs
- 1 tsp vanilla extract
- 250ml sour cream

Instructions:

1. Preheat the oven to 180°C (350°F). Combine graham cracker crumbs, melted butter, and sugar, and press into a springform pan. Bake for 10 minutes, then cool.
2. Melt chocolate and set aside.
3. Beat cream cheese and sugar until smooth. Add eggs one at a time, then stir in vanilla and sour cream.
4. Pour the mixture over the crust. Swirl melted chocolate into the cheesecake batter.
5. Bake for 50–60 minutes until set. Let cool, then refrigerate for at least 4 hours.

Chocolate Pudding

Ingredients:

- 200g dark chocolate
- 500ml whole milk
- 100g sugar
- 2 tbsp cornstarch
- 1 tsp vanilla extract
- Pinch of salt

Instructions:

1. In a saucepan, heat milk and sugar until warm.
2. In a bowl, whisk cornstarch and a little milk until smooth. Slowly add this mixture to the warm milk while stirring constantly.
3. Stir in chocolate and cook over medium heat until thickened.
4. Remove from heat, add vanilla and salt, and whisk until smooth.
5. Pour into serving dishes and refrigerate for 2-3 hours before serving.

Chocolate-Dipped Pretzels

Ingredients:

- 200g dark chocolate
- 12–15 pretzel rods or twists
- Sprinkles or sea salt for garnish (optional)

Instructions:

1. Melt the chocolate in a heatproof bowl over simmering water.
2. Dip each pretzel into the melted chocolate, coating it halfway.
3. Place the dipped pretzels on parchment paper and sprinkle with sea salt or sprinkles.
4. Let the chocolate set in the fridge for about 30 minutes before serving.

Chocolate-Peanut Butter Cups

Ingredients:

- 200g dark chocolate
- 100g peanut butter
- 2 tbsp powdered sugar

Instructions:

1. Melt chocolate in a heatproof bowl over simmering water.
2. Mix peanut butter and powdered sugar until smooth.
3. Spoon a layer of melted chocolate into muffin liners, then a spoonful of peanut butter, and cover with more chocolate.
4. Refrigerate for 1-2 hours until firm.

Chocolate-Pecan Pie

Ingredients:

- 1 pie crust (store-bought or homemade)
- 200g dark chocolate
- 150g pecan halves
- 200g corn syrup
- 100g sugar
- 4 large eggs
- 2 tbsp butter, melted
- 1 tsp vanilla extract
- Pinch of salt

Instructions:

1. Preheat the oven to 180°C (350°F).
2. Melt chocolate and set aside.
3. In a bowl, whisk together eggs, sugar, corn syrup, melted butter, vanilla, and salt.
4. Stir in melted chocolate and pecans. Pour into the pie crust.
5. Bake for 40–45 minutes, until the filling is set. Let cool before serving.

Chocolate-Coconut Bars

Ingredients:

- 200g dark chocolate
- 1 cup shredded coconut
- 200g sweetened condensed milk
- 100g graham cracker crumbs

Instructions:

1. Preheat the oven to 180°C (350°F). Line a baking dish with parchment paper.
2. Mix shredded coconut, sweetened condensed milk, and graham cracker crumbs together.
3. Press the mixture into the baking dish.
4. Melt chocolate and pour over the coconut mixture.
5. Refrigerate for 2-3 hours, then cut into bars.

Chocolate-Dipped Marshmallows

Ingredients:

- 200g dark chocolate
- 12–15 marshmallows
- Sprinkles, crushed nuts, or sea salt (optional)

Instructions:

1. Melt the chocolate in a heatproof bowl over simmering water.
2. Insert a toothpick or skewer into each marshmallow.
3. Dip each marshmallow into the melted chocolate, coating halfway.
4. Roll in sprinkles, crushed nuts, or sea salt, if desired.
5. Place on parchment paper and refrigerate for 30 minutes to set.

Chocolate Meringue Pie

Ingredients:

For the crust:

- 200g graham cracker crumbs
- 100g melted butter
- 2 tbsp sugar

For the filling:

- 200g dark chocolate
- 250ml whole milk
- 3 large egg yolks
- 100g sugar
- 2 tbsp cornstarch
- 2 tbsp butter
- 1 tsp vanilla extract

For the meringue:

- 3 large egg whites
- 150g sugar
- 1 tsp vanilla extract

Instructions:

1. Preheat the oven to 180°C (350°F). Combine the graham cracker crumbs, melted butter, and sugar, and press into a pie dish. Bake for 10 minutes, then cool.
2. For the filling, melt the chocolate in a saucepan. In another bowl, whisk milk, egg yolks, sugar, and cornstarch. Gradually add this mixture to the melted chocolate and cook until thickened. Stir in butter and vanilla.
3. Pour the filling into the cooled crust.
4. For the meringue, beat egg whites and sugar until stiff peaks form. Spoon the meringue onto the filling and bake for 10-12 minutes until golden.
5. Let cool before serving.

Chocolate Pots de Crème

Ingredients:

- 200g dark chocolate
- 500ml heavy cream
- 100g sugar
- 4 large egg yolks
- 1 tsp vanilla extract

Instructions:

1. Preheat the oven to 160°C (325°F).
2. Melt chocolate in a heatproof bowl over simmering water.
3. In a saucepan, heat cream and sugar until warm.
4. Whisk egg yolks and slowly pour in the warm cream mixture, stirring constantly.
5. Pour the mixture into small ramekins and bake in a water bath for 20–25 minutes until set.
6. Refrigerate for 2-3 hours before serving.

Triple Chocolate Cake

Ingredients:

For the cake:

- 200g all-purpose flour
- 100g cocoa powder
- 1 tsp baking powder
- 1 tsp baking soda
- 200g sugar
- 3 large eggs
- 240ml milk
- 120ml vegetable oil
- 1 tsp vanilla extract
- 200g dark chocolate, melted

For the ganache:

- 200g dark chocolate
- 200ml heavy cream

For the frosting:

- 200g white chocolate
- 200ml heavy cream

Instructions:

1. Preheat the oven to 180°C (350°F). Grease and line two 9-inch cake pans.
2. Mix flour, cocoa powder, baking powder, baking soda, and sugar in a bowl.
3. Add eggs, milk, oil, vanilla, and melted chocolate. Mix until smooth.
4. Pour into prepared pans and bake for 25-30 minutes.
5. For the ganache, heat cream and pour over chopped chocolate. Stir until smooth.
6. For the frosting, heat cream and pour over chopped white chocolate, stirring until smooth.
7. Frost the cake with ganache, then drizzle with white chocolate frosting.

Chocolate Croissants

Ingredients:

- 1 sheet puff pastry
- 100g dark chocolate, chopped
- 1 egg (for egg wash)
- Powdered sugar (optional)

Instructions:

1. Preheat the oven to 200°C (400°F).
2. Roll out the puff pastry and cut it into triangles.
3. Place a few pieces of chocolate on the wide end of each triangle.
4. Roll them up into croissant shapes.
5. Brush with egg wash and bake for 15-20 minutes, or until golden.
6. Dust with powdered sugar before serving, if desired.

Chocolate Almond Biscotti

Ingredients:

- 200g all-purpose flour
- 100g sugar
- 2 large eggs
- 1 tsp vanilla extract
- 100g almonds, chopped
- 100g dark chocolate, chopped
- 1 tsp baking powder
- ½ tsp salt

Instructions:

1. Preheat the oven to 180°C (350°F). Line a baking sheet with parchment paper.
2. Mix flour, sugar, baking powder, and salt in a bowl.
3. Beat eggs and vanilla, then mix into the dry ingredients.
4. Stir in almonds and chopped chocolate.
5. Shape dough into a log and bake for 25 minutes.
6. Slice into pieces and bake for an additional 10-12 minutes, turning halfway through.

Chocolate Babka

Ingredients:

For the dough:

- 500g all-purpose flour
- 7g dry yeast
- 100g sugar
- 2 large eggs
- 120ml milk
- 1 tsp vanilla extract
- 100g butter, softened

For the filling:

- 200g dark chocolate, melted
- 100g sugar
- 1 tsp cinnamon

For the syrup:

- 100g sugar
- 100ml water

Instructions:

1. In a bowl, combine flour, yeast, sugar, eggs, milk, and vanilla. Knead into a dough and let rise for 1-2 hours.
2. Roll out dough and spread with melted chocolate, sugar, and cinnamon.
3. Roll into a log, twist, and place into a greased loaf pan. Let rise for 30 minutes.
4. Preheat oven to 180°C (350°F) and bake for 25–30 minutes.
5. For the syrup, heat sugar and water until dissolved, then pour over the babka once it's out of the oven.

Chocolate Chip Scones

Ingredients:

- 250g all-purpose flour
- 100g sugar
- 1 tsp baking powder
- 1 tsp vanilla extract
- 120g butter, cold
- 100g chocolate chips
- 2 large eggs
- 150ml milk

Instructions:

1. Preheat the oven to 200°C (400°F) and line a baking sheet with parchment paper.
2. Mix flour, sugar, and baking powder in a bowl.
3. Cut butter into the dry ingredients until the mixture resembles breadcrumbs.
4. Add chocolate chips, eggs, and milk, and stir until combined.
5. Shape the dough into a round disc and cut into wedges. Bake for 15-18 minutes.

Chocolate Peanut Butter Pie

Ingredients:

For the crust:

- 200g graham cracker crumbs
- 100g melted butter
- 2 tbsp sugar

For the filling:

- 200g dark chocolate
- 100g peanut butter
- 100g sugar
- 250g cream cheese, softened
- 250ml whipped cream

Instructions:

1. Preheat the oven to 180°C (350°F). Press graham cracker crumbs into a pie dish and bake for 10 minutes. Let cool.
2. Melt chocolate and peanut butter together.
3. In a separate bowl, beat cream cheese and sugar until smooth. Stir in melted chocolate and peanut butter.
4. Fold in whipped cream and pour into the cooled crust.
5. Refrigerate for 4 hours before serving.

Chocolate Hazelnut Mousse

Ingredients:

- 200g dark chocolate
- 100g hazelnut spread
- 300ml heavy cream
- 1 tsp vanilla extract

Instructions:

1. Melt chocolate in a heatproof bowl over simmering water.
2. Stir in hazelnut spread until smooth.
3. Whip heavy cream until stiff peaks form, then gently fold into the chocolate mixture.
4. Spoon mousse into serving glasses and refrigerate for at least 2 hours.

Chocolate Caramel Brownies

Ingredients:

For the brownie batter:

- 200g dark chocolate (70% cocoa)
- 100g butter
- 200g sugar
- 3 large eggs
- 1 tsp vanilla extract
- 100g all-purpose flour
- ½ tsp baking powder
- Pinch of salt

For the caramel layer:

- 200g brown sugar
- 100g butter
- 200ml heavy cream
- 1 tsp vanilla extract

Instructions:

1. Preheat the oven to 180°C (350°F). Grease and line a baking pan.
2. Melt chocolate and butter together in a heatproof bowl over simmering water.
3. Whisk eggs, sugar, and vanilla, then fold in the melted chocolate. Stir in flour, baking powder, and salt.
4. Pour the brownie batter into the prepared pan and bake for 20–25 minutes.
5. For the caramel, heat brown sugar, butter, and cream in a saucepan, stirring until smooth. Simmer for 5 minutes.
6. Pour the caramel over the baked brownies and refrigerate for 1–2 hours before slicing.

Chocolate and Raspberry Tart

Ingredients:

For the crust:

- 200g digestive biscuits or graham crackers, crushed
- 100g melted butter
- 2 tbsp sugar

For the filling:

- 200g dark chocolate
- 200ml heavy cream
- 1 tsp vanilla extract

For the raspberry layer:

- 1 cup fresh raspberries
- 2 tbsp sugar

Instructions:

1. Preheat the oven to 180°C (350°F). Combine the crushed biscuits, melted butter, and sugar, then press into a tart pan. Bake for 10 minutes and cool.
2. Melt the chocolate in a heatproof bowl over simmering water.
3. Heat the cream until it just starts to simmer, then pour over the melted chocolate. Stir in vanilla and cool for 10 minutes.
4. For the raspberry layer, mash raspberries with sugar and spread over the cooled crust.
5. Pour the chocolate filling over the raspberries and refrigerate for 2-3 hours. Garnish with fresh raspberries before serving.

Chocolate-Pistachio Tart

Ingredients:

For the crust:

- 200g digestive biscuits or graham crackers, crushed
- 100g melted butter
- 2 tbsp sugar

For the filling:

- 200g dark chocolate
- 100g pistachio paste
- 200ml heavy cream
- 1 tsp vanilla extract

Instructions:

1. Preheat the oven to 180°C (350°F). Combine crushed biscuits, melted butter, and sugar, then press into a tart pan. Bake for 10 minutes and cool.
2. Melt the chocolate in a heatproof bowl over simmering water.
3. Heat the cream in a saucepan until simmering. Add the cream to the chocolate and stir until smooth.
4. Stir in pistachio paste and vanilla, then pour into the cooled crust.
5. Refrigerate for 2-3 hours before serving. Garnish with crushed pistachios.

Chocolate Lava Cookies

Ingredients:

- 200g dark chocolate (70% cocoa)
- 100g butter
- 150g brown sugar
- 1 large egg
- 1 tsp vanilla extract
- 150g all-purpose flour
- ½ tsp baking soda
- Pinch of salt

Instructions:

1. Preheat the oven to 180°C (350°F). Line a baking sheet with parchment paper.
2. Melt chocolate and butter together in a heatproof bowl over simmering water.
3. Whisk sugar, egg, and vanilla, then stir in the melted chocolate.
4. Mix in flour, baking soda, and salt.
5. Spoon the dough onto the baking sheet, shaping it into balls. Bake for 10-12 minutes, leaving the centers soft.
6. Let the cookies cool for 5 minutes, then serve warm to enjoy the gooey centers.

Chocolate Ricotta Cake

Ingredients:

- 250g ricotta cheese
- 200g dark chocolate (70% cocoa)
- 200g sugar
- 4 large eggs
- 1 tsp vanilla extract
- 100g all-purpose flour
- 1 tsp baking powder
- 1 pinch of salt

Instructions:

1. Preheat the oven to 180°C (350°F). Grease and line a springform pan.
2. Melt chocolate in a heatproof bowl over simmering water.
3. Beat ricotta, sugar, eggs, and vanilla until smooth. Add the melted chocolate and mix well.
4. Stir in flour, baking powder, and salt.
5. Pour the batter into the prepared pan and bake for 40-45 minutes, until set.
6. Let it cool before serving, dusted with powdered sugar.

Chocolate Churros

Ingredients:

For the churros dough:

- 200g all-purpose flour
- 1 tsp baking powder
- 1 tsp salt
- 200ml water
- 100g butter
- 2 large eggs
- 1 tsp vanilla extract

For the chocolate dipping sauce:

- 200g dark chocolate
- 200ml heavy cream
- 1 tsp vanilla extract

For rolling:

- 100g sugar
- 1 tsp cinnamon

Instructions:

1. Heat water and butter in a saucepan until it melts. Add flour, baking powder, and salt. Stir until smooth.
2. Remove from heat and stir in eggs and vanilla until fully combined.
3. Heat oil in a frying pan for deep frying. Pipe churros into the oil and fry until golden brown.
4. For the sauce, melt chocolate and cream in a heatproof bowl over simmering water. Stir in vanilla.
5. Roll churros in sugar and cinnamon, then serve with chocolate dipping sauce.

Chocolate Banana Bread

Ingredients:

- 2 ripe bananas, mashed
- 200g dark chocolate, chopped
- 200g all-purpose flour
- 100g sugar
- 1 tsp baking soda
- ½ tsp salt
- 2 large eggs
- 120ml vegetable oil
- 1 tsp vanilla extract

Instructions:

1. Preheat the oven to 180°C (350°F). Grease a loaf pan.
2. Mix mashed bananas, eggs, oil, and vanilla in a bowl.
3. In another bowl, whisk flour, sugar, baking soda, and salt.
4. Stir the dry ingredients into the banana mixture, then fold in chopped chocolate.
5. Pour the batter into the loaf pan and bake for 50-60 minutes, until a toothpick comes out clean.

Chocolate Tiramisu

Ingredients:

- 200g dark chocolate
- 250g mascarpone cheese
- 250ml heavy cream
- 100g sugar
- 2 tsp vanilla extract
- 200g ladyfingers
- 100ml espresso or strong coffee
- 1 tbsp cocoa powder

Instructions:

1. Melt chocolate in a heatproof bowl over simmering water.
2. Beat mascarpone, heavy cream, sugar, and vanilla until smooth. Stir in melted chocolate.
3. Dip ladyfingers in espresso and layer them in a serving dish.
4. Spread a layer of the chocolate mascarpone mixture over the ladyfingers.
5. Repeat layers, then refrigerate for at least 4 hours. Dust with cocoa powder before serving.

Chocolate-Coffee Cake

Ingredients:

For the cake:

- 200g all-purpose flour
- 100g cocoa powder
- 1 tsp baking powder
- 1 tsp baking soda
- 1 tsp salt
- 100g sugar
- 100g brown sugar
- 2 large eggs
- 240ml milk
- 120ml vegetable oil
- 1 tsp vanilla extract
- 120ml brewed coffee

For the frosting:

- 200g dark chocolate
- 200ml heavy cream
- 1 tsp vanilla extract

Instructions:

1. Preheat the oven to 180°C (350°F). Grease and flour a cake pan.
2. Whisk together flour, cocoa powder, baking powder, baking soda, and salt.
3. In another bowl, mix sugar, brown sugar, eggs, milk, oil, vanilla, and brewed coffee until smooth.
4. Gradually add the dry ingredients to the wet ingredients, mixing until combined.
5. Pour the batter into the prepared pan and bake for 25-30 minutes.
6. For the frosting, heat heavy cream until it just starts to simmer, then pour over chopped chocolate. Stir until smooth.
7. Let the cake cool, then frost and serve.

Chocolate and Mint Cupcakes

Ingredients:

For the cupcakes:

- 200g all-purpose flour
- 100g cocoa powder
- 1 tsp baking powder
- 1 tsp baking soda
- ½ tsp salt
- 200g sugar
- 2 large eggs
- 120ml vegetable oil
- 240ml milk
- 1 tsp vanilla extract
- 1 tsp peppermint extract

For the frosting:

- 200g dark chocolate
- 100g butter
- 2 tbsp heavy cream
- 1 tsp peppermint extract

Instructions:

1. Preheat the oven to 180°C (350°F). Line a muffin tin with cupcake liners.
2. Whisk together flour, cocoa powder, baking powder, baking soda, and salt.
3. In another bowl, mix sugar, eggs, oil, milk, vanilla, and peppermint extract.
4. Gradually add the dry ingredients to the wet ingredients, mixing until smooth.
5. Fill the cupcake liners with batter and bake for 18–20 minutes.
6. For the frosting, melt chocolate and butter together in a heatproof bowl. Stir in heavy cream and peppermint extract.
7. Frost the cupcakes once they've cooled and serve.

Chocolate Coconut Macaroons

Ingredients:

- 200g shredded coconut
- 200g dark chocolate (70% cocoa)
- 2 large egg whites
- 100g sugar
- 1 tsp vanilla extract
- ½ tsp salt

Instructions:

1. Preheat the oven to 180°C (350°F). Line a baking sheet with parchment paper.
2. Beat egg whites, sugar, vanilla, and salt until stiff peaks form.
3. Gently fold in shredded coconut.
4. Scoop spoonfuls of the coconut mixture and shape into small mounds on the baking sheet.
5. Bake for 15-20 minutes until golden brown.
6. Melt chocolate in a heatproof bowl over simmering water. Dip each macaroon into the chocolate and let set.

Chocolate Layer Cake

Ingredients:

For the cake:

- 200g all-purpose flour
- 200g cocoa powder
- 1 tsp baking powder
- 1 tsp baking soda
- 1 tsp salt
- 200g sugar
- 200g brown sugar
- 2 large eggs
- 240ml milk
- 120ml vegetable oil
- 2 tsp vanilla extract
- 240ml boiling water

For the frosting:

- 200g dark chocolate
- 250g butter, softened
- 200g powdered sugar
- 1 tsp vanilla extract
- 2 tbsp milk

Instructions:

1. Preheat the oven to 180°C (350°F). Grease and line two 9-inch cake pans.
2. Mix flour, cocoa powder, baking powder, baking soda, and salt in a bowl.
3. In another bowl, whisk sugar, brown sugar, eggs, milk, oil, and vanilla. Gradually add the dry ingredients and mix well.
4. Stir in the boiling water (the batter will be thin).
5. Pour the batter into the prepared pans and bake for 30-35 minutes.
6. For the frosting, melt chocolate in a heatproof bowl. Beat butter until fluffy, then add powdered sugar, melted chocolate, vanilla, and milk.
7. Frost the cooled cake and serve.

Chocolate Fudge Brownies with Walnuts

Ingredients:

- 200g dark chocolate (70% cocoa)
- 100g butter
- 200g sugar
- 3 large eggs
- 1 tsp vanilla extract
- 100g all-purpose flour
- ½ tsp baking powder
- Pinch of salt
- 100g walnuts, chopped

Instructions:

1. Preheat the oven to 180°C (350°F). Grease and line a baking pan.
2. Melt chocolate and butter together in a heatproof bowl over simmering water.
3. In a separate bowl, whisk sugar, eggs, and vanilla. Stir in the melted chocolate mixture.
4. Fold in flour, baking powder, and salt. Add chopped walnuts and mix.
5. Pour the batter into the pan and bake for 20-25 minutes.
6. Let cool before cutting into squares and serving.

Chocolate Soufflé Cake

Ingredients:

- 200g dark chocolate (70% cocoa)
- 100g butter
- 150g sugar
- 3 large eggs
- 1 tsp vanilla extract
- 100g all-purpose flour
- 1 tsp baking powder
- Pinch of salt

Instructions:

1. Preheat the oven to 180°C (350°F). Grease and flour a cake pan.
2. Melt chocolate and butter together in a heatproof bowl over simmering water.
3. Whisk sugar, eggs, and vanilla in another bowl until smooth.
4. Stir in the melted chocolate mixture, then add flour, baking powder, and salt.
5. Pour the batter into the pan and bake for 25-30 minutes. The center should be slightly soft.
6. Let cool for a few minutes before serving.